HORSE & PONY

HORSE & PONY

THE COMPLETE GUIDE TO RIDING & PONY CARE

JANE HOLDERNESS-RODDAM

PHOTOGRAPHY *by* BOB LANGRISH

igloo

Published in 2008
by Igloo Books Ltd.
Cottage Farm
Sywell
NN6 OBJ
www.igloo-books.com

10 9 8 7 6 5 4 3 2 1

ISBN 978-1-84817-291-3

Designed by The Bridgewater Book Company

Printed and manufactured in China

Contents

Introduction

Dealing with horses and ponies in the correct way is very important, and it must be recognized that while being wonderful companions and friends, they are also very aware of what is going on around them and so will be quick to react to certain situations. Most experienced ponies are well behaved with people but, because they are herd animals by nature, they can react unpredictably in a crowd or if frightened. Children should always be supervised when handling horses, particularly if there are other animals around.

This book explains what is involved with learning to ride and how to get started, as well as the basics of how to properly look after a pony or horse. It also outlines what equipment you will need and how to use the accepted terminology, and what it means. Understanding a horse's behavior and what he is trying to tell you through his body language is also covered, and the options available to you once you have mastered the art of getting on and off your pony, and you are able to stop, start, and steer during the three main paces of walk, trot, and canter.

Being with horses and ponies at a stable yard, or even with your own animal at home, can be one of the most enjoyable ways to spend your weekend or spare time. Generally, horses love company and enjoy attention and being made to feel special for some of the time during the day.

However, like people, horses also need space and it is important to allow them plenty of peace and quiet. If you think about how you would feel about a particular situation, for example, a sudden loud noise, this can often help you decide if your pony is going to feel the same way. Remember, horses will react to certain situations.

ABOVE The bond between a rider and a pony can become very precious.

This book gives you basic information, but the best way to find out more is to ask as much as you can about horses from people with more experience so that you learn as you go. If you do have problems at any time, do not take risks. Always either get off, if alone, and lead your pony back for help or get help before trying something on your own that you are not sure about.

ABOVE Horse riding is a thrilling experience for both the rider and the horse.

ABOVE RIGHT There's no need for physical strength, just sound training of both horse and rider.

Throughout the book, there are helpful hints to give you extra guidance wherever possible. Although the pony is often used as an example, the information can also relate to those who keep or ride horses. You should bear in mind that a horse is not only bigger but has different traits to ponies, such as being less hardy in some respects and, sometimes, faster, depending on its breeding and type.

Learning to ride opens up a whole new world that will give you some amazing experiences, not only with your horse or pony, but also the people you meet.

ABOVE Remember that horses were originally wild animals, so they need space and a sense of freedom.

Getting started

There is a lot to know about riding but, before you start, you need to understand some basic terms, and what equipment you will need.

Why ride?

Riding is one of the most special and enjoyable sports of all. Not only is it really exciting, but building up a special bond with your equine friend, whether he's a shaggy pony, a sleek horse, or a future Olympic champion, is fulfilling. Because riding requires people and horses to trust and understand each other, the partnership between them can become a very special one.

OVER THE centuries, the horse has played a huge part in the lives of human beings. They have been vital in the production of food, working as farm animals, and as the quickest means of transport on land. They have been in battle with Alexander the Great, Napoleon, Wellington, and many others, who all relied heavily on their horses to win battles. Horses have played a central role in classic novels, such as *Black Beauty* and *National Velvet*; in cowboy stories such as *The Lone Ranger* and *Champion the Wonder Horse*; and even on the screen, starring in movies such as *The Black Stallion* and *Seabiscuit*. And many horses have become sporting legends on the racetrack, such as Cigar, Mill Reef, Secretariat, Red Rum, and Desert Orchid.

SOMETHING FOR EVERYONE

Whatever your reasons for getting involved, riding is a fantastic hobby or sport for people of all ages and abilities. You can decide to trek quietly through wonderful scenery and beautiful landscapes at home, or be adventurous and go abroad on riding breaks designed for all levels and ages. You can take up an equestrian sport, such as dressage, polo, show jumping, eventing, or endurance riding. There are many options to choose from, and you can be as professional or as relaxed as you want to be with your riding.

Whether you just want to be a "happy hacker," enjoying riding as a pleasant pastime, or become seriously involved in one of the Olympic disciplines at the top end, the bond that will build up between you and your horse or pony will become very important. Horses and ponies are understanding, nonjudgmental, and generally very affectionate, and will do their best to please you.

HEALTHY AND FUN

Riding is a healthy sport. You need to have good balance and coordination and high levels of fitness to cope with the exercise of riding a horse. It may look restful, but it takes a lot of concentration and ability to get to the stage of feeling at one with your horse or pony. When you achieve this, there is nothing more special.

Riding with friends is fun. Getting involved in any of the activities at a riding club or riding school is a great way to enjoy yourself. You may even be asked to help out with some of the activities, so you will meet new friends and feel that you are part of the action.

RIGHT Going for rides with a friend is a rewarding way to spend your spare time.

What is involved

Regular riding lessons when you start out will pay off—you'll need them if you are to learn to ride well and build up confidence. However, you need to remember that your body will need a bit of time to tune itself to this new sport, which can be very energetic. Getting on and off the horse is an art in itself but, once you know how to do this, you will progress quickly to the different paces of walking, trotting, and cantering.

BEING ABLE to sit on the back of such a beautiful creature and control and influence how it moves needs courage and skill, which you will only get by learning how to ride. However, most people with reasonable balance will soon feel confident enough to ride around an arena (or ménage) without any assistance, and do various exercises aimed at improving their riding ability. Soon, you will be able to hack out (ride for pleasure in the countryside on tracks or bridleways), or join in activities at the riding school and aim for the next stage.

DEALING WITH ANIMALS

The first thing you need to know is that you are dealing with an animal that has feelings and reflexes, just like you do. He needs to be understood and appreciated, and it is very important to realize that he can be frightened or upset in certain situations. Being aware of this will make a big difference to how your relationship develops; horses and ponies make wonderful companions and friends, and generally love to please, but your instructions to them need to be consistent and clear so that you can build up a real partnership.

RIGHT Riding is all about learning how to stay balanced and to control your horse.

BELOW Going out into the countryside for a ride (or hacking) is best done with a friend so that you feel safe.

Starting out

There are many different ways of getting used to sitting on a horse—you can sit on a friend's pony, or try out the mechanical horses at shows or exhibitions. You can also go to your local riding school and have a trial lesson on a reliable horse or pony, which knows just how to cope with a beginner.

THE MOST important thing is that the horse you ride is right for you. While you can learn on a safe horse at your stables (known as a schoolmaster), once you are independent the horse needs to be a sensible size for you. He also needs to be responsive enough to react to what you are asking, but not so quick or impulsive that you find him difficult to manage. His temperament is the key to a successful partnership.

FINDING A RIDING SCHOOL OR TRAINING YARD

Look around for a good school that is well recommended, either by friends or in the equestrian press. Go to look at it to ensure that it is well run and the staff are welcoming and friendly. Many suppliers of horse riding equipment or veterinarians will also be able to make recommendations.

Watch a lesson if you can, so that you can learn what is involved before booking one for yourself.

Ask a few questions to make sure that the trainers have qualifications and insurance and are experienced in training people to ride. Check that the horses look well cared for and happy. They must have hay or grass and water readily available. The school should look efficient, well run, and neat. Booking your first lesson should be an enjoyable experience.

POSITION IN THE SADDLE

You will need to know the basics about your position in the saddle before you start riding. It is worth looking at what others are doing before trying it yourself, but your trainer will show you what is needed.

LEFT Being led out on a ride for the first time from your riding school is an exciting experience.

YOU SHOULD ALWAYS CHECK THAT:

1. You are sitting tall but relaxed, and are straight and square in the saddle.
2. You are looking up and forward.
3. Your body is held erect but not stiff.
4. Your legs are hanging evenly.
5. Your knees are bent with the stirrups at a comfortable length.

Having them a little short is better than having them too long, to start with.
6. Your arms are hanging naturally with the elbows bent and relaxed, and your hands are holding the reins with the thumbs on top, just above the horse's withers.
7. Your heels are held low with the toes up and pointing slightly outward.

Equipment and safety

There is a great deal of equipment that is required for riding but, when you are starting out, you need only the basics. Once you are riding more seriously, you can buy extra equipment. The most important thing is to ensure that you are riding safely with an appropriate hat, gloves, and boots with a heel.

THE CLOTHES you wear should be strong, practical, and comfortable. It is very easy to get friction sores or rubs, especially on your legs and knees, but riding jeans or jodhpurs are enough to start with because they have extra padding where needed. Gloves are essential, and a well-fitting hat with a safety harness is standard, as are riding boots or shoes with a heel to stop your foot from slipping through the stirrup iron.

Once you have decided to take up riding seriously, you can get extra equipment as shown on the picture opposite. Your riding school will also advise you on what you need, and many will hire out the essentials such as an appropriate riding hat, or have stores that stock all the kit you need to get started.

The equipment the horse needs, known as tack, will also be provided by the riding school (see opposite).

SAFETY HAT

A riding safety skull cap which is fastened securely, should be worn by all young and inexperienced riders.

RIDING HAT

A riding cap without a safety harness is sometimes used in the show ring for specialist events such as dressage (see page 74).

BODY PROTECTOR

Body protectors are generally used for jumping and for young riders until they are more confident and less likely to fall. They come in many different color combinations.

SAFETY

Your own safety and the safety of the horse must always be a top priority. The golden rule is to think ahead, always remembering that the horse can get frightened or startled. Never take unnecessary risks.

RIGHT Safety stirrups allow your foot to come free if you fall off the horse. This stirrup has a rubber band that will release if you fall.

KEY:

1. Safety hat
2. Safety harness
3. Shirt
4. Riding colors
5. Jodhpurs
6. Gloves
7. Pad
8. Saddle
9. Safety stirrups
10. Riding boot
11. Girth
12. Whip
13. Headpiece
14. Browband
15. Cheek strap
16. Noseband
17. Bit
18. Throat lash
19. Reins

Horse terms and what they mean

Before you start riding, it helps to understand something about the horse terminology that is used internationally, although you may find that a few things have different names or descriptions in certain countries or areas.

LEARNING NEW terms is always a bit strange—when you first start out it will seem unfamiliar, but you will soon get to know what the terms are. Certain words will come up frequently, so it's good to start by understanding these.

HORSE VERSUS PONY

Horses and ponies have different characteristics and traits, but as a rough guide, a pony is usually less than 60in (148cm). A horse is generally any height above that.

BREEDS

Horses and ponies may be a specific breed, such as Welsh or Connemara ponies, or perhaps thoroughbreds or Morgans. They will have some specific characteristics that make them instantly recognizable.

There are hundreds of different breeds from different parts of the world, and they vary tremendously in type and size, from the miniature Shetland ponies through to the huge Clydesdales, used for pulling heavy machinery. Some have been bred for a

specific purpose over hundreds of years, with the pedigrees painstakingly recorded over the centuries, such as the thoroughbred horses used for racing.

TYPES

The majority of animals used as riding horses and ponies may be of unknown parentage but can best be described by their type. Some may be chunky and round and are best described as cobs, while a "riding pony type" looks like a miniature thoroughbred but with the characteristics of a pony, and it can excel in a variety of roles. Other types of horses and ponies include hunters and hacks (see page 20-21).

BONE

The amount of bone a horse or pony has is used as a guide as to how much weight he should reasonably be expected to carry for his size. It is measured just below the knee on the cannon bone. An experienced horse person can tell you how to assess this.

TEMPERAMENT

A horse with a kind and willing temperament is priceless. It is very important to be able to enjoy riding a horse. Nothing is more frustrating than being on one who does not want to work for you or spends most of the time trying to get rid of you. This is why it is so important to have a good teacher, especially in the early days, until you are sure of what you are doing and know how to deal with any problems.

THE GAITS

This is a term used to describe the different paces of the horse—walk, trot, canter, and gallop—and is more fully described in the riding section (see pages 28–29).

THE AIDS

This is a term used to describe the way you direct or communicate to your horse what you want him to do. Your legs, seat, voice, and hands work together to tell your horse to go forward, turn, or stop. Artificial aids include the whip and spurs.

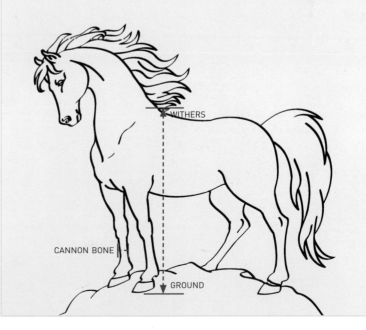

MEASURING

How to measure bone
The amount of bone is measured around the cannon bone, just below the knee. The more bone there is, the stronger the horse or pony is.

How to measure height
The height of horses and ponies is measured in inches/centimeters from the ground to the top of their withers with a measuring stick.

WITHERS

CANNON BONE

GROUND

LEFT Standing side by side it is easy to see the difference between a horse and pony.

Different types and breeds

There are many different types and breeds of horses and ponies. Type refers to general characteristics such as shape and size whereas breed refers to a horse that has particularly obvious characteristics, such as the Arab, with its pretty face shaped like a dish (known as "dished"), flaring nostrils, arched neck, and high flowing tail.

THE PONY

THERE IS a huge variation in types of pony, from miniatures, few of which are strong enough to ride, to some of the native breeds such as the pony of the Americas, the Welsh and the Connemara pony. They share distinct characteristics including a short length of leg relative to the depth of the body. A good temperament is important to help them cope with young riders.

THE COB

This stocky, weight-carrying animal is used by most riding schools because it has a calm and obliging disposition and comes in all shapes and sizes, so there will probably be one to suit your height and weight. Its ancestry is varied and it is often a cross between two heavy type breeds. Cobs often have their manes clipped off because they can become very thick.

LEFT Cobs tend to have kind and gentle dispositions and make ideal riding animals. They are the strongest type of horse for riding.

RIGHT The lighter hack or riding horse is suited for most competitive disciplines once trained.

BELOW RIGHT Palomino horses are distinguished by their golden color and white mane and tail.

BELOW This is a typical hunter type; strong but athletic and capable of carrying some weight. They are generally good jumpers.

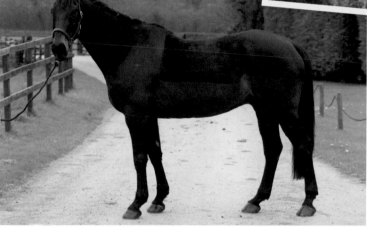

THE HUNTER

This is a strong-boned horse, usually well-mannered, and used to being asked to do different things. Many are good looking enough to do well in the show ring, where there are several classes for them to participate in. These include being led from the ground (known as 'in hand'), being ridden, or being jumped.

THE RIDING PONY

These ponies are small, and can do anything from jumping to mounted games. The ponies are active and energetic, but usually remain calm enough for a young rider to handle. They excel in the show ring, where there are many competitions that cater for them, and they are judged on their looks and performance.

THE HACK

The hack has a lighter frame than the hunter, and is more of a ladies' horse. It should be a straightforward ride and is ideal for most people who want to get started.

THE PALOMINO

This is not a breed or type but rather a horse or pony distinguished by its wonderful golden coat. This, together with its white mane and tail, makes it very popular.

Know your horse

Knowing the different parts of your horse will make riding him more rewarding and will ensure that you are able to understand what others are talking about, so it is worth taking time to learn some of the most common terms and expressions.

THE PARTS OF A PONY OR HORSE

The parts of a pony or horse are collectively known as the points of the horse. The picture below shows some of the main terms you may come across. The left side of the horse is termed the "near side" and the right is known as the "off side." You may hear someone say that you generally get on or mount your horse on the near side or that he is lame on his off foreleg.

COATS

Horses and ponies have many different shades of coat. Some are specific to a certain breed. There is a wide variety and often they will look different in the winter, when they shed their coat for a thicker one to cope with the colder weather.

The main colors are bay—these horses always have black manes, tails, and lower limbs; brown, chestnut or sorrel, gray, palomino, pinto, paint, skewbald, or piebald. It is rare to find a true black or white horse. Grays often have a coat of a completely different color as foals, which then changes to a dark gray. As they get older the coat then fades or becomes paler, usually ending up snowy white.

MARKINGS

The white leg and face markings, if there are any, vary tremendously on every horse but generally fit into one of the recognized categories described:
FACE—blaze, star, stripe, snip, or white face
LEGS—sock, stocking, or white leg
HOOVES—white, black, or striped
Whorls are circular clusters of hair usually found on the head, neck, and many other parts of the body.

BLAZE

STAR

STRIPE

SNIP

STOCKINGS

SOCKS

KEY:

1. Ears
2. Forelock
3. Forehead
4. Eye
5. Cheek
6. Nostril
7. Mouth
8. Muzzle

9. Chin
10. Throat
11. Poll
12. Neck
13. Mane
14. Withers
15. Back
16. Loins

17. Croup
18. Dock
19. Hindquarters
20. Point of hip
21. Point of buttocks
22. Thigh
23. Gaskin
24. Tail

25. Point of hock
26. Fetlock joint
27. Hoof
28. Stifle
29. Flank
30. Ribs
31. Elbow
32. Tendon

33. Pastern
34. Wall of hoof
35. Coronet
36. Cannon bone
37. Knee
38. Forearm
39. Breast
40. Chest

Your equine friend

Understanding the body language of horses and becoming familiar with horse terms is an important part of building a partnership with your pony.

Making friends building a partnership

Whether you ride at a club or with a friend or are even thinking of getting your own horse, it is essential that you start with the right animal for you and your ability. You need a horse of the correct size and temperament, and one who is ready to respond to your stage of training. Do not be tempted to try a flashy animal before you are able to ride. Your trainer will be able to advise you on the correct animal for you.

WHEN CHOOSING a horse, you need to think carefully about what you need because not all animals will be able or willing to perform at the level you need. Some will never want to be reliable jumpers, or be happy to use a bit for dressage, or gallop sensibly in a crowd to do team chasing.

Whether you have a mare (a female horse or pony) or gelding (a neutered-male horse or pony, not a stallion) can sometimes make a difference to the horse's character and behavior. On the whole, mares are cheaper to purchase, but they can be more moody and require rather more understanding and sensitivity than geldings, which are undoubtedly easier to manage. Make sure that you are clear about any possible differences before making a choice.

You must also consider your budget—horses are expensive animals both to purchase and to look after. Make sure you do your research before you buy.

RIGHT Grass seems to take priority here! However, it's always important to give your pony a little extra attention when you can.

BUILDING UP TRUST

Developing a partnership with your horse takes time and patience. Study him carefully and learn what he is trying to tell you. He can communicate through his ears, his expression, his body language, and his willingness to respond to you (see pages 34–35).

Remember that horses learn by repetition, so you need to be consistent in the way you handle them. Call your horse by name and there is every chance he will come to you.

An occasional snack such as a sugar lump is fine but be careful not to spoil your horse so much that he gets annoyed when you do not have anything for him. Horses can get frustrated and may even turn and kick their owners if not handled correctly.

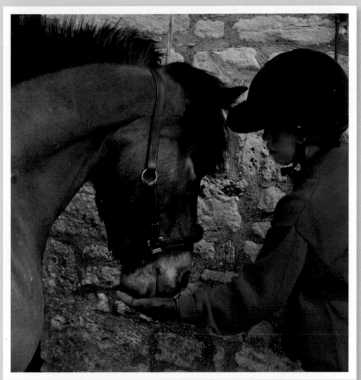

ABOVE Always give any treats from a flat hand to avoid getting your fingers bitten. Be careful not to give too many treats or your pony will start to expect them from you.

Most horses love some attention, especially if they are to be groomed or if they come in for a feed once a day. They will soon learn to be near the gate at the appropriate time. Spending time getting to know your friend and discovering his likes and dislikes is always a rewarding experience. Stroking his coat, feeling the warmth and softness of his muzzle against your hand, and sensing his trust in you and his response to your care is really rewarding.

LEFT Giving your horse time and love will help you to get to know each other.

The gaits
walk, trot, canter, and gallop

There are three main gaits or paces—walk, trot, and canter. The gallop is a fast canter—this is the pace at which racehorses run. You will soon learn which gait is which and, when you ride, will know by feel and balance how to maintain each one.

HOW LONG it will take for you to master each pace will depend on your own confidence and balance, but most riders feel confident at doing a walk and trot after one or two lessons. Feeling confident enough to canter will depend on how quickly you adapt to your pony. Cantering may take a week or two to perfect.

1 Walk is the slowest gait—the horse lifts up each leg independently as he moves forward, so this is a four-beat gait. You will be able to see him do this as he moves if you look carefully. You will feel a slight rocking feeling as he moves forward and you will need to relax and allow your body to move with the pony's steps.

2 In trot, the horse moves his legs in diagonal pairs, springing from one set to the other—this is a two-beat gait. Because of this, the rider finds it easier to rise out of the saddle as the horse changes from one pair of legs to the other. Some horses have a more exaggerated trot than others, so you will feel a greater spring as he moves.

A GALLOPING HORSE

A galloping horse can be very dangerous to someone on the ground, so you should always be aware of what is happening and never be in a position where you can be knocked down.

3 In canter, there are three definite beats as the horse puts down each leg, followed by a moment of suspension. This is called a three-beat gait. When the horse canters on the right rein, his right foreleg will normally lead (as in this picture) and on the left rein, it should be his left foreleg. Most horses tend to be better cantering on one rein, but it is good to practise both.

4 The gallop is a speedy canter, but it becomes four-beat as the horse propels himself forward from each leg as it touches the ground. He stretches his head forward and really moves quickly across the ground.

Catching a horse

When you start to ride, one of the first things you have to learn is how to catch your horse and bring him in from the paddock, or how to go into his stall and tie him up. This involves putting on a head collar or halter, and learning how to lead him safely.

1ST
FOR
CATCHING

ONE OF the most important steps in catching a horse is to keep talking to him to make sure that he knows you are coming toward him. Approach him only from the front and never frighten him with sudden or quick movements.

RIGHT Learn how to do a quick-release safety knot so that in an emergency, you can give one quick pull to set your pony free.

1 Talk to him as you approach slowly, then, when you are alongside, stand still and quietly stroke him. Place the rope over his neck so you can hold onto the horse. Position the nosepiece over his nose, and fasten the strap over his head. Some horses will start to move away as you approach, so take your time and wait for them to come to you.

2 If there are other horses in the field, they might crowd around you, so be sure that you always have another person to help you. Eventually you will feel confident enough catch your horse on your own. Horses can get jealous and may kick out if you are carrying food, so don't do this if there are other horses around.

HOW TO TIE A QUICK-RELEASE SAFETY KNOT

This knot should be tied to a post or rail, or through a ring or another piece of rope. Never tie one to a movable object.

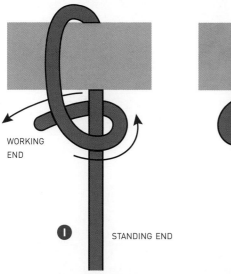

WORKING END

STANDING END

❶

❷

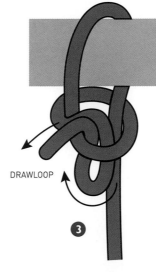

DRAWLOOP

❸

❹

1. Drape the rope or cord over the rail (or through the ring), then take the working end around the back of the standing end.

2. Bring the working end back round to the front and tie an overhand knot (pull the working end through the hole created).

3. Leave a drawloop protruding and do not pull the end completely through the knot.

4. Pull on the loop and the standing end to tighten. To release, pull the end closest to the loop.

3 Lead the horse from the left/near side, holding the rope in your hand in a firm but relaxed manner so that he walks with you at his side. The right hand, nearest the headcollar, should be held just below the clip on the rope for good control. Open the gate or door wide enough to lead him into or out of the stall so that he has plenty of room.

4 To tie up the horse, you need to learn how to tie a quick-release safety knot (see diagram above). This is important in case the horse gets frightened or slips and needs to be freed quickly. It is also possible to buy quick-release fastenings.

Tack and how to fit it

Learning how to tack up your horse is a very exciting step toward becoming a competent rider. However, to start with, the riding school will probably do this for you, until you know more about what is correct and safe.

TIE UP your horse, then collect the tack you need to ride him: a saddle, a pad, a girth of the right size, and a bridle that fits him. It is a good idea to have a martingale or neck strap so that you have a strap to hold onto when you are riding, to help you to keep your balance.

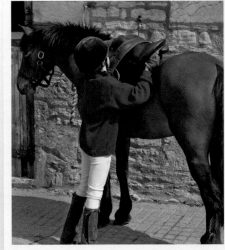

PUTTING ON THE SADDLE

1 Place the pad on the horse's back. Start forward by the withers, then slide the pad back into position.

2 Place the saddle, with the girth attached on the off side and laid over the top of the saddle, on the horse's back and put it in position. Gently lower the girth down the far side and check that it is hanging flat the right way around.

3 Pull the pad up into the front arch of the saddle to stop any pressure on the withers before fastening the girth. This will need to be taken from under the horse's belly, so keep to the side as you do this, and fasten it to the girth straps under the saddle flaps, which are usually to the front, and to the back straps if there are three. Do not fasten too tightly to start with.

PUTTING ON THE BRIDLE AND NECK STRAP

1 Undo the noseband and throat lash on the bridle and hang the bridle over your arm. Place the neck strap or martingale over the horse's head and slide it down the neck. Then take the reins up and over the head onto the neck. Undo the headcollar.

2 Take hold of the main bridle with your right hand and ease the bit into the mouth by placing the finger of your left hand just inside the lip, where there are no teeth, to open the horse's mouth.

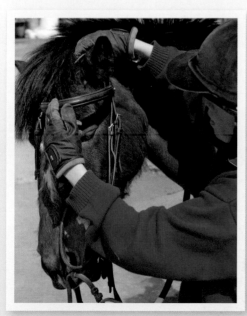

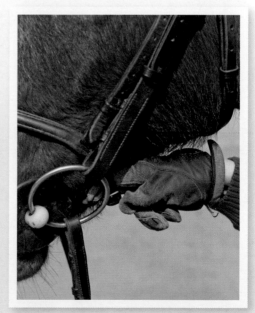

3 Slide the bridle upward and ease one ear at a time gently under the headpiece. Straighten the bridle if necessary and gently pull the forelock out over the browband.

4 Fasten the throat lash, allowing at least a hand's breadth of space between the lash and the horse's cheek to ensure that the lash is not too tightly secured.

5 Fasten the noseband comfortably and straighten anything that is crooked. Check that all keepers (small loops to hold the end of the straps, as on a belt) are secure and safe.

Understanding what your horse is telling you

Horses and ponies can be very expressive, as long as you know how to understand what they are telling you. They communicate with their ears, eyes, how they move, and body language. Take time to learn about how they communicate with you—it may prevent you from having an accident and will help build your relationship.

LOOK AT the eyes—these show fear, alertness, interest, pleasure, or stubbornness if you study them carefully. Knowing how the horse is thinking can help you to handle any problems, because you will know that you need to reassure him with a calming word or gentle pat if he is frightened, or to be firm if he is just being stubborn. Older horses soon learn who they can trick and who they cannot.

The ears also indicate how he is feeling: twitching backward and forward means that he is anxious; laid back flat can indicate aggression or stubbornness; pricked forward may mean pleasure or general interest in what is going on. As you get to know the animal better, you will soon understand what he is telling you.

Body language will also give you a clear indication of what a horse is thinking.

EYES: TRUSTING
A gentle kind eye, such as this one shows a contented outlook, and that he trusts you.

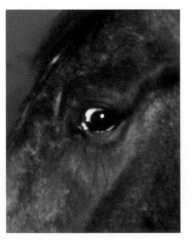

EYES: FEAR/AGGRESSION
A pony showing the whites of its eye may indicate fear or anger.

EARS: ALERT
A calm but interested eye with alert ears show interest and confidence.

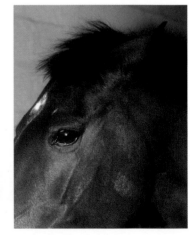

EARS: AGGRESSION
This horse appears unhappy and aggressive as his ears are back—treat with caution.

SIGNS OF STRESS

Weaving—The horse rocks his head from side to side continuously. This is often a sign of stress, although some horses do this only at meal times when they are hungry.

Crib biting—The horse grabs the door or fence with his mouth. A more serious variation of this is called wind sucking, when they grab the door or fence with their mouth and then gulp in air, which can give them belly pain called colic.

Stall walking—The horse walks around and around the stall continuously, as if in a trance. This excessive activity can lead to him losing a lot of his muscle condition.

RIGHT Crib biting may be a sign of stress and can be copied by others. It may also indicate boredom.

ABOVE This pony looks fairly content but not altogether happy with the pressure on his belly.

You need to be careful if he bares his teeth or turns his back on you. This is a definite indication for you to leave his space—he wants to be alone. Sometimes, it works better if you approach him, and then wait for him to come to you. Never hurry. Try to figure out what works best with each horse.

Some people never get along well with animals, while others seem to find it easy. However, by trying to understand a horse's likes and dislikes, you can usually get along with your equine friend pretty well.

However tempted you are to pay attention to your horse, if he clearly wants to be left to himself, then respect that and try not to force him to do something; there are always several other horses who will love receiving as much care and attention as you can give them.

Coping with problems

When you are riding your horse, take note of how he reacts to his surroundings, and you will soon get to know if certain things worry him. Though most horses are not too upset by noise, you may find that your horse reacts to smells or unusual objects.

1ST
FOR
PROBLEM
COPING

THE MOST important thing to remember is to keep calm, don't panic, and try to work out what is worrying your horse. Then you can decide how to cope.

The horse may be frightened of something, such as a particular smell. Horses are very sensitive and may be extremely wary of anything that looks dangerous, such as an odd-shaped log, or something with a strong smell.

1 Napping is when the horse refuses to respond to your aids to go forward, and either plants himself or reverses. It may be caused by your inexperience or it might just be that the horse is testing you. Firmness and perseverance usually work, but losing your temper won't.

2 Rearing can be a frightening experience for any rider. The best thing to do is keep your weight forward and grab the mane for security. It can be caused by the rider being too strong on the rein or can be a reaction to a fright. Try turning in a circle after he has put his front legs down and then tactfully ask the horse to go forward without making too much of an issue of the situation.

A soothing word and some reassurance will usually calm him down. Give the horse time to figure out the problem for himself—it is important to remember he has a brain, too, and his basic instincts need to be considered. He is a "fright-and-flight" animal by nature, although people have come to expect a horse to do what we want all the time.

Napping, rearing, bucking, and bolting are the most common problems, but you can be reassured that these behaviors are unlikely to be a found with a riding school horse, as they are chosen for their docile nature and are used to their surroundings. However, because riding is a partnership of two living creatures working together, there are bound to be times when the unexpected can happen. Being prepared and knowing what to do if your pony reacts in a strange way will help you to cope with anything at any time.

3 Bucking requires good balance and an ability to get the horse's head up quickly. It is much more difficult for him to buck if you keep a firm grip to keep his head up. Bucking is usually caused by natural exuberance—simply letting him loose in a paddock to let off steam may calm him down. Bucking can also be caused by an uncomfortable saddle or girth, or it may tell you that the horse is in pain. It may also be the horse's idea of a joke—if so, you need to be very firm and strong and work him hard so that he doesn't try it again.

4 Bolting is a frightening experience because the horse can gallop off out of control. This may be the result of a fright or because others have galloped off and the horse wants to follow. You must not panic but try, if possible, to slow him down by making him run a circle, shortening the reins, and giving him a lot of reassurance. Lead him back to the school if you think it might happen again, and ask for advice.

First riding lessons

Now it's time to master the basics of getting on and off your pony, walking, trotting, changing direction, and going out for rides.

Getting on and off

The first time you ride is a very special experience. Once you have been on your horse or pony, you will want to progress quickly. However, mastering the art of getting on and off is very important. There are different ways to do this, depending on what you prefer and the facilities that are available to you.

IT IS certainly easier to mount for the first time on a small horse so, if you have a choice, go for the smaller one. Everyone should start by mounting from the ground, because this is the basic way that you need to learn, but it is also possible to mount from a mounting block or to be given a leg-up by a helper.

GETTING ON

To get on a horse, you must have a helper to hold him still until you can do this with ease. Make sure your girths are tight enough and that the stirrups are down before you start. Your trainer will do this for you at first, but you need to get into the habit of checking and knowing what is needed from the start.

1 Start by facing the horse on the near side, take hold of the reins with your left hand, and take hold of the stirrup with your right hand. Lift your left leg up into the stirrup, swivel yourself around to face the saddle, and push upward off the ground, easing your weight on the stirrup iron.

2 Lift your right leg high enough to clear the back of the saddle and the horse, then lower yourself gently into the saddle.

3 Find the right iron—put your right foot into the stirrup on the right of the pony when mounted and settle yourself centrally in the saddle. Take the reins in both hands and check that you feel comfortable and ready. You may need to get someone to adjust the length of the stirrups before moving off.

GETTING OFF

Getting off the horse takes a lot less effort than getting on. You will probably walk around the school or ménage a few times at this first lesson, but it is definitely worth mounting two or three times to get this right before you move on to more exciting activities. Talk to your trainer about how you feel in the saddle and think about whether you feel relaxed and in balance.

LEFT It is important to get the feel of sitting in the saddle and checking the length of your stirrups.

1 First halt and have your trainer hold the horse. Take both feet out of the stirrups and lean forward.

2 Swing your right leg up over the horse's back and gently slide to the ground, holding onto the stirrup leather for balance if necessary.

3 Bend your knees to land and pat the horse.

Fit to ride

You may find riding easy and hear people calling you a "natural," or you may find it more difficult. If you find it hard, working on your fitness will make everything easier.

RUNNING, CYCLING, swimming, walking, and other sports activities are very good for building up physical fitness. Very often, it is not that you are not fit enough, but that you are not allowing yourself to breathe naturally. The body needs oxygen to work properly. You must relax mentally and allow yourself to breathe normally so that you can do the exercises properly. Once you are able to breathe normally while sitting on and managing your horse, you will probably find that you are doing well.

You may become a little stiff to start with, as your body gets used to the change of exercise, but this stiffness will disappear as your muscle tone improves. Be careful not to overdo things, but build up gradually over a few weeks. Riding is a strenuous exercise and one of the few that really uses all your muscles. It also helps with balance, coordination, and concentration, and uses almost every nerve, sense, and brain cell that you possess.

Now that you know a little of what is involved in the sport, you need to think carefully about what you want to achieve and whether you have the time to ride more seriously. Unless you can give enough time to the sport, there is no point in dreaming about being a top showjumper or pleasure rider. You may be happier to be a part-time rider, riding at club level and having a lot of fun and success in a huge variety of equestrian activities.

LEFT Riding is a tough sport and you need to be healthy and fit to become a serious rider.

RIGHT Western riding is extremely popular and requires great skill and training.

Going out for a ride

Once you are confident and happy that you are able to control and steer your horse, think about going out for a ride. Hacking, as it's called, down rural tracks, close to nature, or even out on a road, is exciting. You and your horse are a team; you can make your own decisions, dream your dreams, or just enjoy the experience in your own way.

YOU SHOULD always go with someone else on your first few outings so that there is someone to help you in case of any unexpected problems. It can be a lot of fun exploring on your horse or hacking with friends. If it is an appropriate area, it may also be the best moment to try a few strides of canter in a straight line rather than on a circle in the school. Your trainer will decide which is best, depending on your horse and the circumstances.

If you are going to canter for the first time, it is best to keep forward in the saddle until you get used to the movement.

The canter is a three-time movement, so it will be smoother than the trot, even though it is faster. The aid to canter is to take a slightly firmer feel on the rein and then ask "with a strong leg," that is, squeeze hard with your legs, for the horse to break into canter. At the same time, let your hands move forward as the horse strikes off, then take them back just enough to keep him balanced with enough "leg" to maintain the canter.

If you ride out on roads, you must be aware of your responsibilities and the rules of the road. You need to be visible to be safe. Make sure that you are wearing fluorescent clothing or that your horse is wearing fluorescent bands. It is sometimes difficult to understand why drivers seem to frighten horses by driving too fast but, in many cases, they really do have a problem seeing you, particularly if you are coming around a blind bend. Be aware of this—it is fine to ride two abreast on quiet tracks and roads but not if you are on a twisting or busy road.

FAR LEFT The rider on the right has a fluorescent stripe on her jacket which is important if you are riding out, especially at dusk.

BELOW AND BELOW LEFT Going out for a ride is a great experience on your own or with a friend for company.

First rides out

The first time you go out for a real ride as part of the group, rather than as a beginner, you'll feel special. There are some wonderful places to go riding, but you will have to take responsibility for what you do and act appropriately, so watch what is going on and make sure there are no safety issues.

EVERY RIDER in a horse-riding group needs to ride sensibly on roads, and to be aware of the other riders since good group control is vital. Horses are herd animals and, if one takes off, the rest will try to follow, so everyone must know what the boundaries are as far as speed is concerned.

Respect the countryside so that you make yourself welcome. Most people will welcome you over their land if you ask. Remember to close gates and ride slowly past other animals. Do not ride on growing crops—you will soon be warned off if you damage them.

To go on a more formal ride, there are numerous options available such as a local trail ride or sponsored ride, trek or even a nearby riding break for a few days. You can usually find details in the riding section of your local newspaper, or in a saddlery.

There are many organizations to help you—the Pony Club is a world-renowned youth organization with several branches in most countries. Riding clubs are also popular and most areas will have a club nearby and can be contacted for information. Their websites will provide almost everything you need to set you off in the right direction.

DOS AND DON'TS

Do use reflective clothing if you are riding in the evening or on a dark day.

Do keep your horse's head looking away from anything he may shy away from.

Do avoid icy roads if possible and leave the horse's head free so that he can find his feet if he slips.

Do take your feet out of the stirrups in slippery conditions so that if the horse falls over you can keep your legs up, out of the way.

Don't panic if anything goes wrong—just think about how to cope.

Don't be persuaded to do things you do not feel ready to handle.

Don't forget to thank anyone who helps you—you may need them again.

LEFT Competing in sponsored rides will help you to gain new experience, but make sure you respect the countryside.

RIGHT You must be aware of other people in your group when you go riding out with others.

Jumping simple fences position over fences and coping with problems

To be able to jump simple fences as a course, you need to be able to help by staying balanced as your horse jumps. It is important to ensure that you help instead of hindering him by maintaining a flowing forward and balanced pace into the fence.

AT THIS stage of riding, never attempt anything that is too big for either of you, and make sure you give yourself enough space to approach the fences straight.

There are several different fences, but they generally come into three main categories: uprights, spreads, and combinations.

In training, a series of athletic exercises over poles and fences in a line are called grids. These are very good for building up the athletic ability of the horse or pony. It is important that the striding is suitable for the size of the pony and the type of fences used. They should only be set up by an experienced person.

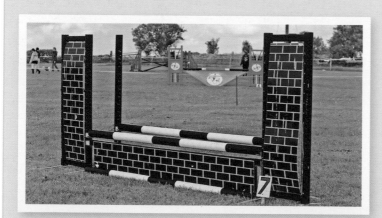

SPREAD FENCE
A spread is a fence with a width that varies in presentation—it may be two rails of the same height, such as a parallel, or it may be a sloping fence, such as a triple bar, or some other variation. As the fences get bigger, the gap underneath will be filled with different types of filler. This one has a wall filler.

COMBINATION FENCE
Combination fences usually have two or three elements. A combination of two fences with one or two non-jumping strides in between is called a double, while three fences is called a treble.

UPRIGHT FENCE

An upright is a single fence without any width to it, which may be small, medium, or large. It is the simplest of the three to jump at the lower height.

Riding cross-country fences

Cross-country riding is one of the most exciting of all equestrian sports and is a real test of horsemanship at its best. Horse and rider must trust each other completely to tackle all kinds of fences, and to ride up and down valleys and hills and across fields.

SAFETY IS a priority, so it is very important that both horse and rider have had enough experience at the beginning stages before going on to the next one. You must learn to go at cross-country speed, which is somewhere between a strong canter and a gallop, in a good, easy rhythm that is nicely balanced. If you go too fast, you will wear out your horse before the end of the course and, if you go too slowly, he will not be able to jump the fences.

The fences are usually solid in construction and are as natural as possible, although logs and natural hedge fences, ditches and rails, banks, and steps up or down have now been joined by artificial boxes, corners, narrow brushes, and walls, as course builders come up with more ideas.

To start your cross-country training, it is a good idea to go with a more experienced friend who can jump over the fences to show you how it should be done. Then you can try. If you are riding a young or inexperienced horse, it may be helpful to follow a friend around for a few fences if your horse is lacking a little in confidence but, if he has done enough jumping, this should not bother him.

As with all fences, sit up and ride forward into them and maintain a forward, well-balanced rhythm during your course. Try to think of it from the horse's point of view—you may know what you are jumping, but he doesn't, so give him the best chance of seeing the fences by riding straight and at the right pace to be able to negotiate them safely. Wider fences need strong riding to make it easier for the animal to negotiate, while upright and narrow fences need more controlled riding to give the horse time to see them.

LEFT Start off with a simple fence to build both the rider's and the horse's confidence.

Do not jump into water too fast, because the drag of the water can unbalance your horse. Jumping uphill or on to banks requires plenty of power and impulsion (pushing the horse forward). Watch how more experienced riders do it and, if they look good and safe, copy how they do it.

BELOW Team chasing is a lot of fun. A team, usually of four experienced riders, competes around a course of cross-country fences.

What to do now you can ride

There are many options open to you as a rider, from competing in shows or the more competitive sports to going on trekking vacations —the choice is yours.

Available options what to enjoy

Riding gives you a great choice of activities that are suitable for all abilities, ages, and ambitions. For the less ambitious, the more attractive activities may be trekking, riding trips, and endurance riding at the pleasure ride stage. Dressage or reining (see page 73) are excellent sports for perfectionists who do not like faster work or jumping. Mounted games, and sports, such as polo and handball, are very competitive.

THE OLYMPIC sports of showjumping, eventing, and top-level dressage are breathtaking to watch as the riders put on amazing displays of horsemanship. For riders with a disability, Disabled Sports USA or the Riding for the Disabled Association in Britain, ensures there is plenty available, and many of their riders have gone on to compete at the Paralympic Games.

TREKKING AND RIDING TRIPS

To go on a trek or riding trip or safari is a great adventure. You ride through beautiful countryside, enjoying the scenery, either over a few days or on one-day treks. It is a great way to meet new friends, or you can go with a few of your own riding friends. Dude ranch holidays let you experience ranch life first hand. There are instructional vacations, family vacations, and specially organized trips. Make sure you know exactly what you will be doing, check out your insurance, and be sure you know what kit and clothing to take.

LEFT Trekking is a great way to enjoy beautiful countryside either at home or abroad.

ABOVE Mounted games are very competitive and a great way to increase balance, control, and coordination.

ABOVE RIGHT Western riding can best be described as Western dressage. Tremendous skill and patient training is required from horse and rider.

REINING

Reining is one of the most popular of the Western classes and originates in some of the movements used by ranch horses. It is generally described as Western dressage and requires a high degree of training of the horse and understanding by the rider. There are a variety of movements, such as walk ins, roll backs, spins, and lead changes, which need patient teaching and great ability on the part of the rider.

MOUNTED GAMES

Mounted games will help you to gain balance, control, and athleticism on your horse. They are usually organized through the Pony Club and are a lot of fun for young people all over the world. You need a fast and obedient animal that responds quickly but does not get too excited. Being able to vault on and off your horse is essential for most of the games, which involve such activities as sack races, spoon races, and barrel or bending races. There are generally two types of game: those that need speed and those that need precision.

PONY CLUB AND RIDING CLUB ACTIVITIES

Many riders join a local pony club or riding club, which organize a wide range of activities for members. Some clubs have team or individual competitions, which are fun and fairly local. The Pony Club is one of the biggest youth organizations in the world and caters for several sports, including mounted games, polo, dressage, eventing, and showjumping. It gives instructional help to all its members. Achieving a pass at any Pony Club test is highly respected internationally.

Where to look for information how to get involved

The best way to decide what you want to get involved in, is to find out what is happening locally and go watch. You should be able to find magazines on riding or a riding section in the local newspaper that has information. Every equestrian sport has a governing body to register members and set the rules for the different categories. Find out where to contact these—they will give you information.

IT IS always best to go watch an activity, to familiarize yourself with what is involved, or to find someone who is already doing it, so that you will be well informed before deciding to try the activity yourself. There may be particular equipment you need, but this can very often be borrowed or hired until you are certain you want to join.

Your local riding school will probably have most of the information you need and may already participate in several different activities. Your trainer can tell you something about most activities but, if he is not involved in the sport himself, you may need to find your information somewhere else.

BEING PART OF A TEAM

It can be fun to learn about the various sports, and it's a great way to make new friends. Even if you don't want to get involved, you can help a brother or sister or adult to take part in a sport they enjoy. It is good to be part of the back-up team for an endurance rider or eventer. There is a lot to do, so you will be part of a team that makes it all work; this can be very exciting and satisfying.

First, you often have to start the rider off in one spot and then dash over with all the necessary equipment to another spot. Then, the horse may need refreshing with a quick wash down, a drink, and a veterinarian check before horse and rider are off on their journey again. After that, you may then have to take all the equipment to the next checkpoint.

ABOVE LEFT Competing in any discipline is fun, but it is always worth finding out what is required before trying one yourself.

GROOM FOR A DAY

Being groom for a day to a friend can also be fun. You will be very involved in everything from tacking up and polishing the horse or pony, ready for its competition, to helping the rider with getting ready to do a certain phase, calming her nerves and generally being there to do whatever is needed.

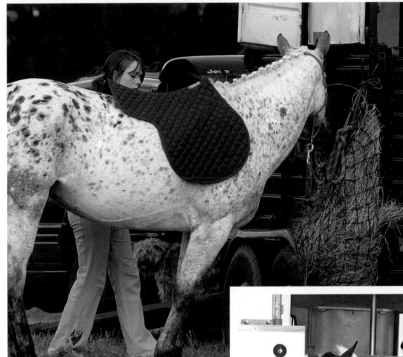

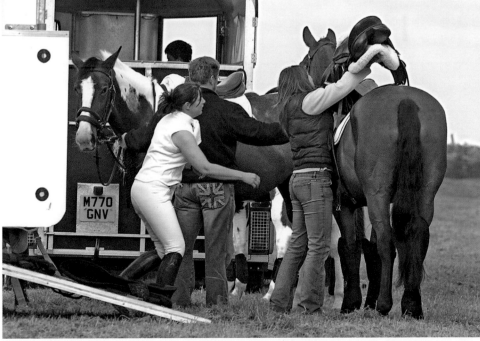

ABOVE Watching and waiting your turn or watching a friend compete can be a nerve-racking experience.

ABOVE Being groom for the day is really exciting but getting everything ready on time can be a challenge.

RIGHT Making sure the day goes well requires everyone to work as a team.

Looking after your horse

Taking care of a horse or pony is a major commitment and it is important that you know how to do it properly.

Know what is involved owning your own horse

It can be difficult to decide whether you can manage to have your own horse or pony. Owning one requires a lot of time and commitment—you cannot leave him if you go away. However, there are other options that you can think about.

SOMETIMES IT is possible to share a horse with a friend so that you can share the responsibilities. You may also adopt or loan a horse at a riding stable—you can look after him in return for lessons if the owner allows this, or you can keep him at a livery yard, but look after him yourself.

If you are sharing a horse or have him on loan, then it is important that a responsible adult signs an agreement to make it clear who is responsible for what. Adults should also consider whether to get insurance, because veterinarian fees can quickly add up to become very expensive.

BELOW Owning your own pony is a wonderful experience, but only if you are able to keep him in appropriate conditions.

WHERE TO KEEP YOUR HORSE

Is your horse going to live out in a paddock all the time or be stabled, with daily exercise? Have you got the appropriate facilities? Is your fencing safe and stockproof? Is there freely available fresh water? If any of these elements are missing, you may not have the amenities to keep a horse.

If you are able to keep your horse in a paddock you will need between 1¼–2½ acres (½–1 hectare) of land per horse, depending on the quality of the grass and the type of horse you are keeping. Horses can manage well on their own but they love company so, if a companion is available, you will need extra land to cater for two.

The paddock needs to be safely fenced with a padlock on the gate. Check the field carefully to make sure there are no sharp objects that might cause injury, and that there are no poisonous plants growing there. "Skip out" or clear the field regularly of horse droppings, to help prevent worm infestations. You will also need to "rest," or keep horses off the paddock periodically to allow regrowth, or fence off half of the paddock until the grass has regrown. Fresh water must always be available.

Shelter from the sun or the weather is essential. This may be provided by a field shelter or by trees and hedges, which can be just as effective. Sometimes a waterproof horse rug can be used in really wet or cold weather for horses with very fine coats, but horses with thick coats usually do not need one.

You may already have a stable to keep him in, and this should be safe and secure, and have a tie ring.

ABOVE New Zealand waterproof rugs keep horses and ponies warm and dry during the winter months.

ABOVE Security can be a problem in some areas, so be sure all paddocks and gates are kept secure.

ABOVE Skipping out paddocks is one of the very necessary chores associated with keeping ponies and horses.

ABOVE Making sure your pony is secured safely when you are grooming or mucking out is vital.

Food and water

Feeding your horse is a skill that comes with experience, but there are a few basic rules. What your horse needs to keep him fit and healthy will depend on his age and condition, his type, and what he does.

A HORSE is used to grazing naturally, with a continuous amount of grass trickling into his stomach. This regime should be adhered to as closely as possible, regardless of what he is doing or where he is. The horse has a small stomach, so he cannot tolerate large amounts all at once, but needs a regular intake of roughage, such as grass or hay, to maintain a healthy digestion.

The horse's work, or lack of it, will decide whether you need to supplement his diet with concentrates, also known as hard feed, to give him the extra energy needed for more energetic work. His diet should consist of a balance of roughage and concentrates. Roughage should always be the main ingredient.

Some horses need more food than others to keep in good condition and some need a restricted diet to prevent obesity. Other things can affect the health of your horse, such as having a lot of worms, poor teeth, or some infections.

EXAMPLES OF ROUGHAGE	EXAMPLES OF CONCENTRATES
Hay	Mixes
Grass	Cubes/Pellets
Haylage	Oats
Chaff/Chop	Barley/Grain
Alfalfa	Maize
Silage	Sugar beet

Alfalfa   Pellets   Coarse mix   Oats

GUIDELINES FOR FEEDING A HORSE OR PONY

There are certain common guidelines for feeding a horse or pony, which are relevant to all types.

1 Feed little and often—this is more natural for the horse. If he is fed concentrates, this can be divided into two or three feeds, with hay or grass in between.

2 Water must be freely available at all times—make sure clean water is available in a field or in his stable. Two buckets may be necessary in hot or very dry conditions, and these may need filling at least two or three times during the day.

3 Make any changes to the diet slowly over a period of several days. Any sudden changes to a horse's diet can cause colic (belly pain), which can be fatal.

4 Use only good quality feed—this may seem obvious, but you must check that your horse food is not musty or out of date and is of good quality. Fussy feeders may prefer a different brand.

5 The main ingredient—at least 60 percent—must be roughage, depending on how much hard feed is being added to make up the energy requirements required for competition or schooling. Remember that horses and ponies are browsing animals and need some roughage most of the time to keep their gut healthy.

6 Feed according to the work being done. Always cut down the food if the horse is not being worked, to prevent a build-up of protein in his system.

7 Be consistent and weigh food. Both hard food and roughage should be weighed to ensure you are giving the same amounts every day.

8 Never exercise your horse too soon after feeding. Allow at least one hour for digestion.

Horse health

A healthy horse should have bright eyes and a glossy coat, even though it may be muddy or greasy in the field. He should look cheerful and have a sense of wellbeing. His temperature, pulse, and breathing should be regular and he should be in good condition, neither too fat nor too thin.

YOUR HORSE is sick if he looks unusually lethargic, has a dull coat and eye, feels particularly hot and is breathing fast, is sweating abnormally, is kicking at his stomach or rolling (which could indicate colic), is streaming mucus from his nostrils and has swollen glands, especially around the neck, and looks generally unwell. You should call the veterinarian immediately. Always have the phone number available and a set of directions on how to find your horse.

BELOW AND OPPOSITE TOP
A healthy horse will be alert with bright eyes and a shiny coat.

BEST KEPT HORSE

LAMENESS

Most lameness problems can be attributed to the foot. Abscesses can be very painful for the horse because the horn cannot expand when there is inflammation. A bruised or punctured sole may be relatively minor, but it will be more serious if the bone structures in the foot have been affected. If a stone gets lodged in the foot, it can cause severe lameness but, once it has been removed, the problem is usually solved.

Other problems can be caused by strains to tendons, which are always serious, bruising, muscle strains, bone degeneration of varying degrees, or trauma such as a bad cut.

VACCINATIONS, WORMING, AND TEETH CARE

All horses need to be on a regular worming program to keep them healthy. They are vulnerable to worms because they ingest worm larvae from the grass. Your veterinarian will recommend a suitable regime, depending on where you are and the time of year. Other horses using the same land should be on the same schedule.

Vaccinations vary from country to country, but influenza and tetanus, which can be deadly to horses and ponies, are essential everywhere. You need to keep an official record of these. Your veterinarian will advise you on what other vaccinations are necessary. Certain states have different requirements and, sometimes, there are outbreaks of equine diseases that have to be controlled through vaccination.

Your horse will have to have his teeth rasped, or filed, at least once a year by a veterinarian or equine dentist. This will make sure that his teeth stay in good shape and that he can chew his food properly.

ABOVE Lameness in the foot is common. Look out for stones lodged between the frog (the V-shaped area shown above) and shoe.

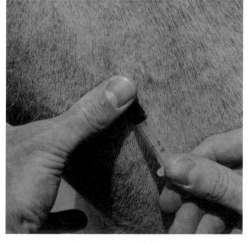

ABOVE Vaccinations vary from country to country, but anti-flu and tetanus are universal for all equines.

ABOVE Worming needs to be carried out three or four times annually. Ask your veterinarian for advice on what to use.

Rugs and when to use them

Nature provided horses and ponies with winter and summer coats that change with the seasons. Left to their own devices, they adapt to the weather and produce enough grease in their coats to keep warm and dry. However, because people feel it is necessary to interfere with nature, we have to provide a variety of different covers to protect horses.

BRUSHING AND washing the grease out of horses' and ponies' coats means that they feel the cold much more and cannot stay dry when it rains. Rugs become a necessity in these conditions if the horse is stabled and does not have a very thick coat. There are many different rugs to choose from but, generally, the lightest rug for the weather conditions is best. Check that it has good strong fastenings and is the right size for your horse.

If your horse is out in bad weather, it is possible to get a waterproof outdoor rug. Again, the lightest for the conditions is usually best. Heavy thick rugs restrict movement and hinder rather than help an animal that is used to being free. It is worth getting two of each type of rug so that you can change them if they get too soiled or wet. If a rug has leg straps, they should be cross-fastened to ensure the legs do not get chafed or rubbed.

LEFT Outdoor waterproof rugs come in a variety of different designs, so look for one that is the right size for the horse and as light as possible with good strong fastenings.

TYPES OF RUGS

There is a huge selection of special rugs and sheets.

• A fly sheet is very fine and lightweight and more or less envelops the whole animal, which will appreciate this if the flies are bad.

• Waterproof sheets are wonderful to have with you if you are competing or otherwise want to keep horse and tack protected from the elements.

• Summer sheets are very lightweight and used to keep the pony clean.

• Fleece or moisture-wicking rugs enable the coat to dry but let the moisture through and, so, reduce the likelihood of the horse catching a chill.

Most rugs and sheets now have cross-over fastenings. Make sure they are fastened properly so that there is no chance of the rug or sheet blowing up and frightening the horse. A special string, called a fillet string, should be attached to the back of the rug under the tail. This helps to keep the rug in place so that it doesn't blow up in the wind. These do not always come attached to the rugs, so you may need to buy one separately.

BELOW A fly sheet covers most of a horse to stop flies becoming too much of a nuisance.

Grooming kit

Grooming is a rewarding activity when looking after your horse. It keeps the horse's coat healthy and clean, removing any mud, dirt, or dried sweat and, generally, gives your horse a good appearance. It is also one of the best ways to bond with your equine friend, because you get to know each other as you go through the various stages on a one-to-one basis.

TOP GROOM

FOR A horse you keep in the field, it is a good idea to brush him off before you ride him, so that his coat is free of mud and dirt. He is less likely to get sore if he sweats under the saddle.

For the stabled horse, a quick brush off before riding, to tidy him up, is usually followed by a more thorough clean once he is dry and back in his stable after exercise.

GROOMING KIT

Dandy brush
To clean mud and dirt on long coats

Body brush
To brush clean and fine coats

Metal curry comb
For cleaning the body brush

Hoof pick and hoof oil
To pick out the feet and oil them

Sponges
For cleaning the eyes, nose, and tail

Rubber curry comb
For removing dirt and mud

Stable rubber
For that final polish

Grooming kit box
To keep everything neat and together

Other useful items for your kit are a sweat scraper for removing excess water after washing the horse down, a water brush for laying the mane down if it is a little unruly, a tail bandage to keep the tail neat, a mane and tail comb for keeping these neat, and a large pair of sharp scissors for trimming whiskers and the end of the tail.

PICKING UP FEET

1 Tie up your horse with a quick-release safety knot (see page 31) in a safe place or in his stable. Start by picking out his feet, one by one, with the hoof pick. Always clear any mud or stones carefully (as shown). Most horses will quickly learn to pick up their feet for you if you stick to a set system of lightly tapping them on the side of the leg you are dealing with, or running your hand down that leg.

BRUSHING

2 If the horse is dirty or has a long winter coat, rub the coat all over using a rubber curry comb or dandy brush to remove any loose hair or mud, avoiding any sensitive parts or the head. If he has his fine summer coat, this process should be done with a body brush, using the metal curry comb to clean the brush. Pay special attention to the head, brushing well behind the ears and down the back of the throat.

SPONGING

3 Take the sponge, wring it out with water, and sponge around his eyes, nose, and under his tail, being careful to lift this up gently while standing to the side. You can also wash off any bad stains, if necessary.

FINAL POLISH

4 Brush the mane or separate the strands by hand and give the coat a final polish with a stable rubber. Never brush the tail except when holding the end, because it will pull out the hairs, but the tail can be separated by hand, if necessary.

OILING THE FEET

5 Oil the feet with an oil brush two or three times a week.

Boots and bandages, on the move

Boots and bandaging are generally designed for protection, and there are many different types designed to protect every part of the horse. It is, however, pointless to clutter your horse up with all these unless it is really necessary. If you are taking your horse or pony to a show, make sure you get everything ready well in advance.

A HORSE'S legs are vulnerable to knocks, especially if our horse moves rather "close." This refers to when the pony is likely to brush or hit itself with the opposite leg (thereby causing injury), so brushing boots on the front legs, back legs, or both can be a sensible precaution, especially if you are jumping. Look for light but strong boots that are easy to put on and take off, with strong fastenings.

Overreach or bell boots help prevent injury if the horse's hind legs clip the back of the front heels, because this can be painful and cause soreness. These boots come in various styles,

ranging from the pull-on type to thicker and chunkier versions. Travel boots have more or less replaced the bandage, and protect the legs from the knees and hocks downward. They are specially designed for when the horse is in a trailer, but they need to be the right size or they tend to slip.

Other boots are designed for specific uses, such as open-fronted for jumping, ankle boots to protect the fetlocks, speedy-cut for the high stepper (a horse that is likely to hit itself further up the leg), and several others. Ask your saddler to recommend a design.

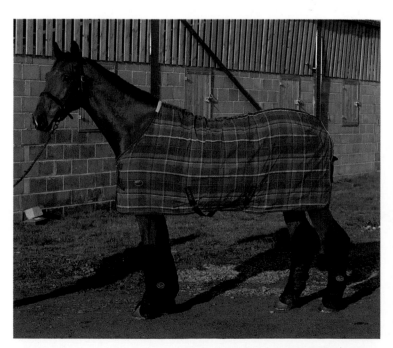

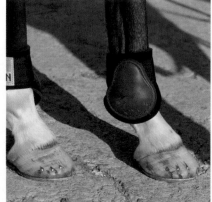
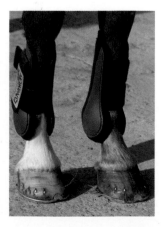

LEFT Traveling equipment includes protective travel boots, rug, tail bandage, and head collars with lead rope. Rugs are chosen according to the weather.

BELOW Hind brushing boots (left) prevent rubbing and open-fronted brushing boots (below) protect the tendons from injury.

GOING TO A SHOW

When you go on an outing, it is important that your horse is as well presented as you are. Not only does he need to look neat, clean, and well polished, but you will need the right equipment for him.

Make a list of what you need and be sure it gets packed in the trailer or truck. Think about the time it takes to get there and how much time you will need to collect your competition numbers, walk a course, and get yourself and your horse ready and warmed up for whatever activity you are about to do. You should always have someone with you at a competition in case you need help or something goes wrong.

Make sure your own equipment is ready and that you have directions, rules, and schedules and any membership cards you may need. Allow plenty of time. A small hay net will help to keep your horse happy for the journey, but do not let him stuff himself if you are expecting him to do lot of fast work on arrival.

BELOW Horses and pones should be tied with safety knots to breakable string on their trailers while they are waiting.

KIT FOR A SHOW

Hay and water
2 buckets
Sponge and scraper
Muck sheet and shovel
Tack
Riding clothes
Food and water for rider
Directions, rules, and schedule

Index

ACKNOWLEDGEMENTS
The Bridgewater Book Company would like to thank iStock photography for permission to use the bottom right image on p21, and also the models Lauren Gibson, Sarah Gibson, Louis Graves, Daisy Sims-Hilditch, Ella Abbott, Kate Raynor, Helen Sizer and Karna Solberg.